A Scottish Poetry Book

compiled by
Alan Bold

illustrated by
Bob Dewar
Iain McIntosh
Rodger McPhail

Oxford University Press   1983

Oxford University Press, Walton Street, Oxford OX2 6DP

London   Glasgow   New York   Toronto
Delhi   Bombay   Calcutta   Madras   Karachi
Nairobi   Dar es Salaam   Cape Town
Kuala Lumpur   Singapore   Hong Kong   Tokyo
Melbourne   Auckland

and associates in
Beirut   Berlin   Ibadan   Mexico City   Nicosia

© Oxford University Press 1983

ISBN 0 19 916030 9 (non net)
ISBN 0 19 916029 5 (net)

Phototypeset by Tradespools Ltd, Frome, Somerset

Printed in Hong Kong

British Library Cataloguing in Publication Data
A Scottish poetry book.
  1. English poetry—Scottish authors
  I. Bold, Alan
  821'.00809411   PR8651

ISBN 0–19–916029–5
ISBN 0–19–916030–9

The publishers would like to thank the following for
permission to reproduce photographs:

Mike Abrahams/Network, p. 107; Barnaby's Picture
Library, pp. 119 and 120/121; BBC Hulton Picture Library,
p. 98; and Barry Lewis/Network, pp. 19 and 86/87.

Contents

sometimes I come

sometimes I come
sometimes I go
but which is which
I don't know

sometimes I am
sometimes I'm not
but which is which
I forgot

R.D. Laing

The Moon

The moon is a boat that drifts in the sky
with nobody near but the stars that stand by
peering down as if they wished to say,
'Who pulled up the anchor and let you away?'

Iain Crichton Smith

The Beast in the Space

Shut up. Shut up. There's nobody here.
If you think you hear somebody knocking
On the other side of the words, pay
No attention. It will be only
The great creature that thumps its tail
On silence on the other side.
If you do not even hear that
I'll give the beast a quick skelp
And through Art you'll hear it yelp.

The beast that lives on silence takes
Its bite out of either side.
It pads and sniffs between us. Now
It comes and laps my meaning up.
Call it over. Call it across
This curious necessary space.
Get off, you terrible inhabiter
Of silence. I'll not have it. Get
Away to whoever it is will have you.

He's gone and if he's gone to you
That's fair enough. For on this side
Of the words it's late. The heavy moth
Bangs on the pane. The whole house
Is sleeping and I remember
I am not here, only the space
I sent the terrible beast across.
Watch. He bites. Listen gently
To any song he snorts or growls
And give him food. He means neither
Well or ill towards you. Above
All, shut up. Give him your love.

W.S. Graham

Come Sailin'

Come intil my boat
I'll tak ye for a sail,
We'll mebbe catch a cod
A mackerel or a whale,
We'll mebbe catch a mermaid
And we will be enthralled
But I think it far mair likely
We'll only catch the cauld.

J.K. Annand

The Three Voyages
(and a prayer)
of Captain Cook

```
                    h
                    m
                    s
        e n d e a v o u r
        e n d e a v o u r
      e n d e a v o u r
      e n d e a v o u r
      e n d e a v o u r
        e n d e a v o u r
                    h
                    m
                    s
        r e s o l u t i o n
        r e s o l u t i o n
      r e s o l u t i o n
      r e s o l u t i o n
      r e s o l u t i o n
        r e s o l u t i o n
                    h
                    m
                    s
        d i s c o v e r y
        d i s c o v e r y
      d i s c o v e r y
      d i s c o v e r y
      d i s c o v e r y
        d i s c o v e r y
                    o
                    g
                    o
                    d
```

SAILSETFORTHEGRE
ATSOUTHLANDAND
MAYTHEVOYAGE
BEFRUITFUL

Alan Riddell

Crab

All his savings are sunk in his claws.
Like frightened roots sprung out of his head
His eyes pop out on everlasting stilts.
When he walks, he is a six-legged plant,
Fortifications on top, and rock back,
Supplies safeguarded, a real crab.

J.F. Hendry

Sir Patrick Spens

The king sits in Dumferling toune,
　Drinking the blude-reid wine:
'O whar will I get guid sailor,
　To sail this schip of mine?'

Up and spak an eldern knicht,
　Sat at the kings richt kne:
'Sir Patrick Spence is the best sailor
　That sails upon the se.'

The king has written a braid letter,
　And signed it wi' his hand,
And sent it to Sir Patrick Spence,
　Was walking on the sand.

The first line that Sir Patrick red,
　A loud lauch lauched he:
The next line that Sir Patrick red,
　The teir blinded his ee.

'O wha is this has done this deid,
　This ill deid don to me,
To send me out this time o' the yeir,
　To sail upon the se?!

'Mak hast, mak hast, my mirry men all,
　Our guid schip sails the morne:'
'O say na sae, my master deir,
　For I feir a deadlie storme.

'Late late yestreen I saw the new moone,
  Wi' the auld moone in hir arme,
And I feir, I feir, my deir master,
  That we will cum to harme.'

O our Scots nobles were richt laith
  To weet their cork-heild schoone;
Bot lang owre a' the play wer playd,
  Thair hats they swam aboone.

O lang, lang, may their ladies sit,
  Wi' thair fans into their hand,
Or eir they se Sir Patrick Spence
  Cum sailing to the land.

O lang, lang, may the ladies stand,
  Wi' thair gold kems in their hair,
Waiting for their ain deir lords,
  For they'll se thame na mair.

Have owre, have owre to Aberdour,
  It's fiftie fadom deip,
And thair lies guid Sir Patrick Spence,
  Wi' the Scots lords at his feit.

Anon.

The Seagull

The seagull, favourite of poets, sails above the bridge,
its craw stuffed with whitening worms.

Scanner,
its head moves from side to side in the wind.

Up there it sees nothing but the gullworld of wires,
crisscrossing girders and the shoal of waves.

Up there it hears nothing but the whirr in its dirty
feathers, the squawk in its beak, the thud of gusts.

Strung on the wind, it twirls: lifting, sour,
feeling its mass of worms move.

Tom Buchan

Catfish

The leopard eye of a murderer
and the body of an eel
combine to form a velvet glove
that has a grip like steel.

J.F. Hendry

The Famous Tay Whale

'Twas in the month of December, and in the year 1883,
That a monster whale came to Dundee,
Resolved for a few days to sport and play,
And devour the small fishes in the silvery Tay.

So the monster whale did sport and play
Among the innocent little fishes in the beautiful Tay,
Until he was seen by some men one day,
And they resolved to catch him without delay.

When it came to be known a whale was seen in the Tay,
Some men began to talk and to say,
We must try and catch this monster of a whale,
So come on, brave boys, and never say fail.

Then the people together in crowds did run,
Resolved to capture the whale and to have some fun!
So small boats were launched on the silvery Tay,
While the monster of the deep did sport and play.

Oh! it was a most fearful and beautiful sight,
To see it lashing the water with its tail all its might,
And making the water ascend like a shower of hail,
With one lash of its ugly and mighty tail.

16

Then the water did descend on the men in the boats,
Which wet their trousers and also their coats;
But it only made them the more determined to catch the
    whale,
But the whale shook at them his tail.

Then the whale began to puff and to blow,
While the men and the boats after him did go,
Armed well with harpoons for the fray,
Which they fired at him without dismay.

And they laughed and grinned just like wild baboons,
While they fired at him their sharp harpoons:
But when struck with the harpoons he dived below,
Which filled his pursuers' hearts with woe:

Because they guessed they had lost a prize,
Which caused the tears to well up in their eyes;
And in that their anticipations were only right,
Because he sped on to Stonehaven with all his might:

And was first seen by the crew of a Gourdon fishing boat,
Which they thought was a big coble upturned afloat:
But when they drew near they saw it was a whale,
So they resolved to tow it ashore without fail.

So they got a rope from each boat tied round his tail,
And landed their burden at Stonehaven without fail:
And when the people saw it their voices they did raise,
Declaring that the brave fishermen deserved great praise.

And my opinion is that God sent the whale in time of need,
No matter what other people may think or what is their
    creed;
I know fishermen in general are often very poor,
And God in His goodness sent it drive poverty from their
    door.

So Mr John Wood has bought it for two hundred and
   twenty-six pound,
And has brought it to Dundee all safe and all sound;
Which measures 40 feet in length from the snout to the tail,
So I advise the people far and near to see it without fail.

Then hurrah! for the mighty monster whale,
Which has got 17 feet 4 inches from tip to tip of a tail!
Which can be seen for a sixpence or a shilling,
That is to say, if the people all are willing

William McGonagall

18

The Seagull

Seagull, seagull, sit on the sand,
It's never good weather when you're on the land.

Anon.

Me

I'm the original
Plasm o' the ocean
Feebly amused
At God's last notion

He ettles to use me
Like a conjurer's hat
And gar me evolve
He disna ken what—

Countries wi' their flora
And fauna—but lor!
He forgets hoo often
He's dune it afore.

I couldna thole
The process again
If he didna aye think
It has juist dawned on his brain,

If he didna aye wonder
Hoo faur he could cairry it
—Losh me when he canna
As muckle as vary it!

I'm the original
Plasm o' the ocean;
Humour accoonts
For my ditherin' motion.

Hugh MacDiarmid

Basking Shark

To stub an oar on a rock where none should be,
To have it rise with a slounge out of the sea
Is a thing that happened once (too often) to me.

But not too often—though enough. I count as gain
That once I met, on a sea tin-tacked with rain,
That roomsized monster with a matchbox brain.

He displaced more than water. He shoggled me
Centuries back—this decadent townee
Shook on a wrong branch of his family tree.

Swish up the dirt and, when it settles, a spring
Is all the clearer. I saw me, in one fling,
Emerging from the slime of everything.

So who's the monster? The thought made me grow pale
For twenty seconds while, sail after sail,
The tall fin slid away and then the tail.

Norman MacCaig

21

Ballad of the Flat Earth

This is the tale of the Markinel,
  An idiot ship was she;
She went hurtling over the edge of the world
  Thinking it round, you see.

The ruddy skip of this mighty ship
  (Which was built in the river Clyde)
Thought the world was a great big beautiful sphere
  With an atmosphere outside.

He told his crew what they had to do
  On their maiden voyage: *well*,
They planned to sail once round the world
  To test the Markinel.

On the fateful day it was anchors-a-weigh,
  It was batten-down-the-hatch;
It was port-to-starboard – all these terms
  That seadogs have to watch.

The skipper bored all the men aboard
  With his yards and yards of yarn;
He told them jokes, he showed them maps
  (For skippers never learn).

He said he'd found the world was round
  (A globe, a ball, a sphere)
Or, rather, had been *told* it was:
  'Things ain't what they appear.'

As if heaven-sent the Markinel went
  On her quest for the shape of the earth.
For a while the first mate dozed at his post
  And the skipper kipped in his berth.

As the horizon loomed the captain boomed
  'Right, mates, full steam ahead.'
(Or some such, rather nautical, term;
  At least I *think* that's what he said.)

At the edge of the world the whirlpools whirled
    And the skipper skipped with delight;
But the purser pursed his lips as the ship
    Dropped off into space, into night.

Like the planet Mars, among billions of stars,
    The Markinel floats about space;
Like a figurehead, there at the front of the ship,
    Is the skipper's bright red face.

If, somehow, you could reach him now
    And ask if the world was flat
He would say, 'My friend, well of course it is,
    I fell off, there's your proof, and that's that.'

That was the tale of the Markinel
    And I think you'll agree with me:
No good can come from exploring the skies
    If you don't know what's what in the sea.

Alan Bold

The Rainbow

The rainbow's like a coloured bridge
that sometimes shines from ridge to ridge.
Today one end is in the sea,
the other's in the field with me.

Iain Crichton Smith

25

The Whistle

He cut a sappy sucker from the muckle rodden-tree,
He trimmed it, an' he wet it, an' he thumped it on his knee;
He never heard the teuchat when the harrow broke her eggs,
He missed the craggit heron nabbin' puddocks in the seggs,
He forgot to hound the collie at the cattle when they strayed,
But you should hae seen the whistle that the wee herd made!

He wheepled on't at mornin' an' he tweetled on't at nicht,
He puffed his freckled cheeks until his nose sank oot o' sicht,
The kye were late for milkin' when he piped them up the closs,
The kitlin's got his supper syne, an' he was beddit boss;
But he cared na doit nor docken what they did or thocht or said,
There was comfort in the whistle that the wee herd made.

For lyin' lang o' mornin's he had clawed the caup for weeks,
But noo he had his bonnet on afore the lave had breeks;
He was whistlin' to the porridge that were hott'rin' on the fire,
He was whistlin' ower the travise to the baillie in the byre;
Nae a blackbird nor a mavis, that hae pipin' for their trade,
Was a marrow for the whistle that the wee herd made.

He played a march to battle, it cam' dirlin' through the mist,
Till the halflin squared his shou'ders an' made up his mind to 'list;
He tried a spring for wooers, though he wistna what it meant,
But the kitchen-lass was lauchin' an' he thocht she maybe kent;
He got ream an' buttered bannocks for the lovin' lilt he played.
Wasna that a cheery whistle that the wee herd made?

He blew them rants sae lively, schottisches, reels, an' jigs,
The foalie flang his muckle legs an' capered ower the rigs,
The grey-tailed futt'rat bobbit oot to hear his ain strathspey,
The bawd cam' loupin' through the corn to 'Clean Pease Strae';
The feet o' ilka man an' beast gat youkie when he played—
Hae ye ever heard o' whistle like the wee herd made?

But the snaw it stopped the herdin' an' the winter brocht him dool,
When in spite o' hacks an' chiblains he was shod again for school;
He couldna sough the catechis nor pipe the rule o' three,
He was keepit in an' lickit when the ither loons got free;
But he aften played the truant—'twas the only thing he played,
For the maister brunt the whistle that the wee herd made!

Charles Murray

THE CLOUD'S ANCHOR

swallow

Ian Hamilton Finlay

A Boy's Song

Where the pools are bright and deep,
Where the grey trout lies asleep,
Up the river and o'er the lea,
That's the way for Billy and me.

Where the blackbird sings the latest,
Where the hawthorn blooms the sweetest,
Where the nestlings chirp and flee,
That's the way for Billy and me.

Where the mowers mow the cleanest,
Where the hay lies thick and greenest,
There to trace the homeward bee,
That's the way for Billy and me.

Where the hazel bank is steepest,
Where the shadow falls the deepest,
Where the clustering nuts fall free,
That's the way for Billy and me.

Why the boys should drive away
Little sweet maidens from the play,
Or love to banter and fight so well,
That's the thing I never could tell.

But this I know, I love to play,
Through the meadow, among the hay;
Up the water and o'er the lea,
That's the way for Billy and me.

James Hogg

Today

So here hath been dawning
Another blue day;
Think, wilt thou let it
Slip useless away?

Out of eternity
This new day is born;
Into eternity
At night will return.

Behold it aforetime
No eye ever did:
So soon it for ever
From all eyes is hid.

Here hath been dawning
Another blue day;
Think, wilt thou let it
Slip useless away?

Thomas Carlyle

Requiem

Under the wide and starry sky,
Dig the grave and let me lie.
Glad did I live and gladly die,
    And I laid me down with a will.

This be the verse you grave for me:
Here he lies where he longed to be;
Home is the sailor, home from sea,
    And the hunter home from the hill.

Robert Louis Stevenson

The Black Horseman

'Look out, he's coming.
The black horseman is coming!'
Children run down from the hill,
Wild flowers spill
From their hair and hands.
Down the net-spread sands
The fishermen push out errandless boats.
Only the goats
On the hill, and the cows
Contentedly browse.
Ploughman the furrow has fled, shepherd the fold.
The laird double-locks his chest of onyx and gold.
He's off to his town abode
Quicker than lover or highwayman ever rode.
His wife up behind,
They pass dunghill and dump like scented wind.
Doors are barred, windows shuttered.
'What's all the fuss?' one old man muttered.
'To a gray fire-sider
He's a good friend, that jet-black rider.
Sooner he comes, the better.'
Girls at the bench of cheese and butter
In the great farm
Run here and there with skirls of alarm,
Apple-bright girls
Driven by a shadow to shrieks and swirls.
The calm birds angle and circle and go.
The jaunty scarecrow
Cares not a jot
For the whirling hoof of the stallion of jet.
The preaching man droops here and there,
All DOOM and BEWARE.
A tinker boy
Stands on a rock to see the black horseman go by.
'The black horseman is coming!'
Stones of the hidden hamlet echo the hooves' drumming.
The sun goes dark.
She falters and falls from the blue, the light-drained lark.

George Mackay Brown

Odd Goings-on in Dunfermline Toun

In yon gusty toun on the slope, folk
slip off it, disappear,
gang in an' oot o' doors
fast, like in auld films,
uphill thin man roon corner,
doonhill fat man intae shop,
lassies intae trees,
auld men intae ruins,
rinnin boys intae the grun,
auld wife gangs heilster gowdie
wi' a puckle leaves,
is blawn richt ower the kirk steeple.
John Bell walks straucht through
the shut gates o' Pittendreigh Park,
never heard tell again an' naebody speirs – why?
Just ane thing ye canna dae,
tak' a stroll intae the sea.

George Bruce

A Runnable Stag

When the pods went pop on the broom, green broom,
   And apples began to be golden-skinned,
We harboured a stag in the Priory coomb,
   And we feathered his trail up-wind, up-wind,
   We feathered his trail up-wind—
      A stag of warrant, a stag, a stag,
      A runnable stag, a kingly crop,
      Brow, bay and tray and three on top,
      A stag, a runnable stag.

Then the huntsman's horn rang yap, yap, yap,
   And 'Forwards' we heard the harbourer shout;
But 'twas only a brocket that broke a gap
   In the beechen underwood, driven out,
   From the underwood, antlered out
      By warrant and might of the stag, the stag,
      The runnable stag, whose lordly mind
      Was bent on sleep, though beamed and tined
      He stood, a runnable stag.

So we tufted the covert till afternoon
   With Tinkerman's Pup and Bell-of-the-North;
And hunters were sulky and hounds out of tune
   Before we tufted the right stag forth,
   Before we tufted him forth,
      The stag of warrant, the wily stag,
      The runnable stag with his kingly crop,
      Brow, bay and tray and three on top,
      The royal and runnable stag.

It was Bell-of-the-North and Tinkerman's Pup
   That stuck to the scent till the copse was drawn.
'Tally ho! tally ho!' and the hunt was up,
   The tufters whipped and the pack laid on,
   The resolute pack laid on,
      And the stag of warrant away at last,
      The runnable stag, the same, the same,
      His hoofs on fire, his horns like flame,
      A stag, a runnable stag.

'Let your gelding be: if you check or chide
  He stumbles at once and you're out of the hunt;
For three hundred gentlemen, able to ride,
  On hunters accustomed to bear the brunt,
  Accustomed to bear the brunt,
    Are after the runnable stag, the stag,
    The runnable stag with his kingly crop,
    Brow, bay and tray and three on top,
    The right, the runnable stag.'

By perilous paths in coomb and dell,
  The heather, the rocks, and the river-bed,
The pace grew hot, for the scent lay well,
  And a runnable stag goes right ahead,
  The quarry went right ahead—
    Ahead, ahead, and fast and far;
    His antlered crest, his cloven hoof,
    Brow, bay and tray and three aloof,
    The stag, the runnable stag.

For a matter of twenty miles and more,
  By the densest hedge and the highest wall,
Through herds of bullocks he baffled the lore
  Of harbourer, huntsman, hounds and all,
  Of harbourer, hounds and all—
    The stag of warrant, the wily stag,
    For twenty miles, and five and five,
    He ran, and he never was caught alive,
    This stag, this runnable stag.

When he turned at bay in the leafy gloom,
  In the emerald gloom where the brook ran deep,
He heard in the distance the rollers boom,
  And he saw in a vision of peaceful sleep,
  In a wonderful vision of sleep,
    A stag of warrant, a stag, a stag,
    A runnable stag in a jewelled bed,
    Under the sheltering ocean dead,
    A stag, a runnable stag.

So a fateful hope lit up his eye,
    And he opened his nostrils wide again,
And he tossed his branching antlers high
    As he headed the hunt down the Charlock glen,
    As he raced down the echoing glen,
        For five miles more, the stag, the stag,
        For twenty miles, and five and five,
        Not to be caught now, dead or alive,
        The stag, the runnable stag.

Three hundred gentlemen, able to ride,
    Three hundred horses as gallant and free,
Behind him escape on the evening tide,
    Far out till he sank in the Severn Sea,
    Till he sank in the depths of the sea—
        The stag, the buoyant stag, the stag
        That slept at last in a jewelled bed
        Under the sheltering ocean spread,
        The stag, the runnable stag.

John Davidson

Porcupine

Although they rarely show their features
porcupines are far from spineless creatures.

J.F. Hendry

Prince Marmaduke

A Tale of a Pussy-Cat

Marmaduke rules. He kens O.K.
there's no' a game he canna play.
In this, his ain wee pussy beat,
he's cock o' the green, king o' the street.

A kitten cat, sae braw and sleek,
he'd tell ye this, gin he could speak.
There was a time (and no' lang since)
when Marmie was a *real* prince!

Sitting in state in his pavilion,
he ruled his subjects by the million.
And law and kirk and schule and army
aa peyed their due respect til Marmie!

Ae day, this wicked witch arrived
and, when she saw the kingdom thrived,
it scunnered her. She took her book
and cast a spell on Marmaduke!

'A pussy-cat ye'll be!' she skirled.
'And need tae trauchle through this world.
Ye'll mooch aboot frae street tae street
and hunt the causeys for your meat!'

So there ye are. Is it no' strange?
There's things e'en magic canna change.
The form is different, no' the natur—
Marm's yet a handsome, royal cratur.

Ablow my windae, ilka day
I watch him rin and sport and play.
He's no' as great as he was aince
—but Marmaduke is still a prince!

Marmaduke rules! He kens O.K.
there's no' a game he canna play.
In this, his ain wee pussy beat,
he's cock o' the green, king o' the street!

Donald Campbell

Spelling Game

If the plural of house is houses
and the plural of mouse is mice
why then the plural of grouses
should surely be written as grice

and if the plural of deer is deer
and the plural of fish is fish
then the plural of beer should be beer
and the plural of dish should be dish.

If mouses run over our houses
and eat up our loaves and our scones
why then our lice should be louses
and our phones should be sounded as phons.

Iain Crichton Smith

The Twa Cats and the Cheese

Twa cats aince on a cheese did light,
To which baith had an equal right;
But disputes, sic as aft arise,
Fell out a-sharing of the prize.

'Fair play,' said ane, 'ye bite ower thick,
Thae teeth of yours gang wonder quick:
Let's part it, else lang 'or the moon
Be changed, the kebuck will be done.'
But wha's to do't; they're parties baith,
And ane may do the other skaith.
Sae with consent away they trudge,
And laid the cheese before a Judge:
A monkey with a campsho face,
Clerk to a Justice of the Peace,
A Judge he seemed in Justice skilled,
When he his master's chair had filled;
Now umpire chosen for division,
Baith sware to stand by his decision.
Demure he looks, the cheese he pales,
He prives it good, ca's for the scales;
His knife whops throw't, in twa it fell;
He puts ilk half in either shell:
Said he, 'We'll truly weigh the case,
And strictest Justice shall have place.'
Then lifting up the scales, he fand
The tane bang up, the other stand:
Syne out he took the heaviest half,
And ate a knoost o't quickly aff,
And tried it syne, it now proved light:
'Friend cats,' said he, 'we'll do ye right.'
Then to the ither half he fell,
And laid till't teughly tooth and nail,

Till weighed again it lightest proved.
The Judge wha this sweet process loved,
Still weighed the case, and still ate on,
Till clients baith were weary grown,
And tenting how the matter went,
Cried, 'Come, come, Sir, we're baith content.'
'Ye fools,' quoth he, 'and Justice too,
Maun be content as well as you.'
Thus grumbled they, thus he went on,
Till baith the halves were near hand done:
Poor pussies now the daffine saw
Of gaun for nignyes to the Law;
And billed the Judge, that he wad please
To give them the remaining cheese,
To which his worship grave replied,
'The dues of Court maun first be paid.
Now Justice pleased, what's to the fore
Will but right scrimply clear your score;
That's our decreet, gae hame and sleep,
And thank us ye're win aff sae cheap.'

Allan Ramsay

To a Mouse

Wee, sleeket, cowran, tim'rous beastie,
O' what a panic's in thy breastie!
Thou need na start awa sae hasty
   Wi' bickering brattle!
I wad be laith to rin an' chase thee,
   Wi' murdering pattle!

I'm truly sorry man's dominion
Has broken Nature's social union,
An' justifies that ill opinion
   Which makes thee startle
At me, thy poor, earth-born companion
   An' fellow mortal!

I doubt na, whyles, but thou may thieve;
What then? poor beastie, thou maun live!
A daimen-icker in a thrave
   'S a sma' request;
I'll get a blessin' wi' the lave,
   An' never miss't!

Thy wee bit housie, too, in ruin!
Its silly wa's the win's are strewin'!
An' naething, now, to big a new ane,
  O' foggage green!
An' bleak December's win's ensuin',
  Baith snell an' keen!

Thou saw the fields laid bare an' wast,
An' weary winter comin' fast,
An' cozie here, beneath the blast,
  Thou thought to dwell,
Till crash! the cruel coulter past
  Out thro' thy cell.

That wee-bit heap o' leaves an' stibble,
Has cost thee monie a wearie nibble!
Now thou's turned out, for a' thy trouble,
  But house or hald,
To thole the winter's sleety dribble,
  An' cranreuch cauld!

But Mousie, thou art no thy lane,
In proving foresight may be vain:
The best-laid schemes o' Mice an' Men
    Gang aft agley,
An' lea'e us nocht but grief an' pain,
    For promis'd joy!

Still thou art blest, compar'd wi' me!
The present only toucheth thee:
But och! I backward cast my e'e,
    On prospects drear!
An' forward, tho' I canna see,
    I guess an' fear!

Robert Burns

I dreamt I was a butterfly

I dreamt I was a butterfly
dreaming it was me
it looked into a mirror
there was nothing there to see

'you lie'
        I cried
it woke
        I died

R.D. Laing

The Late Wasp

You that through all the dying summer
Came every morning to our breakfast table,
A lonely bachelor mummer,
And fed on the marmalade
So deeply, all your strength was scarcely able
To prise you from the sweet pit you had made,—
You and the earth have now grown older,
And your blue thoroughfares have felt a change;
They have grown colder;
And it is strange
How the familiar avenues of the air
Crumble now, crumble; the good air will not hold,
All cracked and perished with the cold;
And down you dive through nothing and through despair.

Edwin Muir

The Honey Pot

Alan Riddell

To a Louse

Ha! whare ye gaun, ye crowlan ferlie!
Your impudence protects you fairly:
I canna say but ye strunt rarely,
   Owre gawze and lace;
Tho' faith, I fear ye dine but sparely
   On sic a place.

Ye ugly, creepan, blastet wonner,
Detestet, shunn'd, by saunt an' sinner,
How daur ye set your fit upon her,
   Sae fine a Lady!
Gae somewhere else and seek your dinner,
   On some poor body.

Swith, in some beggar's haffet squattle;
There ye may creep, and sprawl, and sprattle,
Wi' ither kindred, jumping cattle,
   In shoals and nations;
Whare horn nor bane ne'er daur unsettle
   Your thick plantations.

Now haud you there, ye're out o' sight,
Below the fatt'rels, snug and tight,
Na faith ye yet! ye'll no be right,
   Till ye've got on it,
The vera tapmost, towrin' height
   O' Miss's bonnet.

My sooth! right bauld ye set your nose out,
As plump an' gray as onie grozet:
O for some rank, mercurial rozet,
   Or fell, red smeddum,
I'd gie you sic a hearty dose o't,
   Wad dress your droddum!

I wad na been surpriz'd to spy
You on an auld wife's flainen toy;
Or aiblins some bit duddie boy,
   On's wylecoat;
But Miss's fine Lunardi, fye!
   Haw daur ye do't?

O Jenny dinna toss your head,
An' set your beauties a' abread!
Ye little ken what cursed speed
   The blastie's makin!
Thae winks and finger-ends, I dread,
   Are notice takin!

O wad som Pow'r the giftie gie us
To see oursel's as others see us!
It wad frae monie a blunder free us
   An' foolish notion:
What airs in dress an' gait wad lea'e us,
   And ev'n Devotion!

Robert Burns

53

Frogs

Frogs sit more solid
than anything sits. In mid-leap they are
parachutists falling
in a free fall. They die on roads
with arms across their chests and
heads high.

I love frogs that sit
like Buddha, that fall without
parachutes, that die
like Italian tenors.

Above all, I love them because,
pursued in water, they never
panic so much that they fail
to make stylish triangles
with their ballet dancer's
legs.

Norman MacCaig

The Diseased Salmon

I'm gled it's no' my face,
But a fozie saumon turnin'
Deid-white i' the blue bracks o' the pool,
Hoverin' a wee and syne tint again i' the churnin'.

Mony's the face'll turn,
Like the fozie saumon I see;
But I hope that mine'll never be ane
And I can think o' naebody else's I'd like to be.

Hugh MacDiarmid

Jumping Toad

Under the broad flat stone
was a metropolis of ants. By its edge
a toad sat, looking benign and grandmotherly –
it only needed specs.

Suddenly it floppily jumped,
little amateur – and swallowed
an ant that had left its hometown.

The toad caught my eye with a look that said
You didn't think I had it in me, did you?
And I, dumbfounded, went off
whistling *Knees up, Mother Brown.*

Norman MacCaig

56

Hares Boxing

He went out at three in the morning;
couldn't sleep. And closed the gate
and down the path and over
the stile and off across the fields.

A half moon sidled through the trees.
Two hares sat bolt upright in the grass
and swayed and stepped and
stalked each other round and round.

He saw them leap into the air
and fall back uncertainly; and
then they flexed their limbs
and tossed their heads, stopped

dead again, pricked up their ears;
but he stood still in the shadow
of the woods. The two hares closed
and threw the first test punches.

Neither hit. And then they both
reared up and flailed out till
they fell together and backed off
and sat upright again and swayed

and watched. And he watched
and cocked his rifle bolt.
The hares heard nothing so he raised
his elbow, held one hare in his sights.

The hares began another round
up on their hind legs, jabbing
unsteadily. One knocked the other over
with a blow to the side of the head

and sat down quickly; had
surprised itself and waited
for the other to regain composure;
it did so with a rush

and both went tumbling; got up
and bolted off together, leaping
and shoulder charging till
they disappeared along the dyke.

He followed them in his sights
for a little while then eased
the cocked bolt shut and set
the safety catch. He saw

his hands on the trigger-guard
and on the stock like
someone else's hands. They were
much older than he had remembered.

Robin Bell

59

The Ross-shire Hills

What are the hills of Ross-shire like?
Listen. I'll tell you. Over the snow one day
I went out with my gun. A hare popped up
On a hill-top not very far away.

I shot it at once. It came rolling down
And round it as it came a snowball grew.
Which, when I kicked it open, held not one
But seventeen hares. Believe me or not. It's true.

Hugh MacDiarmid

60

Ballad of the Hare and
the Bassethound

The bassethound's a mournful fellow;
long ears that trail along the ground,
a baying voice that's like a cello,
a tail that circles round and round.

Yet bassethounds were bred for chasing,
through France's royal days of old,
the breathless hare, at first outpacing
the hound who, once he snuffed a hold

of the hare's scent, kept slowly clumbering
ditches, branches, burns and fields
till at the end of all his lumbering,
the limping hare, spring broken, yields.

We're civilised. So basset Billy,
his snuffling anchored to the ground,
was amiable, harmless, silly,
seeking for things he never found.

61

One sudden day he bumped his snout on
a lump of fur, a sleeping hare.
Poor Billy gazed with wrinkled doubt on
the creature that returned his stare.

At once the hare sent distance arc-ing
as towards the setting sun he sped
while Billy sat upon his barking
then turned and oppositely fled.

But not for long. The old blood-royal
that courses through a basset's veins
is not a thing for time to spoil,
even when it feeds slow-thinking brains.

His massive paws he pushed before him
and slithered to a skidding halt.
In vain did I command, implore him—
ancestral blood cried out 'Assault!'

So yelping ancient doggy noises,
Billy set off in late pursuit.
Time waits for no such equipoises:
the jinking hare by then had put

two lengthy fields from where he started
and, smalling, breached a hill's horizon,
Billy, essentially kind-hearted,
pulled up with innocent surprise on

his wrinkled features. Body wagging,
he ambled back to where I waited.
With asking eyes he lay there sagging,
face saved and old French honour sated;

as if to say: 'Come on now, praise me
for showing sense; en Français, *sens*;
like you, to kill's a thought dismays me,
so *honi soit qui mal y pense!*'

Maurice Lindsay

To the Houlet
(for Alison)

Houlet I see
You sat in the tree
Materialised out o' the air;
Like a boy
I peer wi' joy
And whisper 'There!' 'There!' 'There!'

Close in our tree
And yet sae free
Agin the sky bricht to the west;
But daurk soon
Aa aroun'
And you then at your very best.

Houlet I see
You sat in the tree
Fat and large and still;
Wee beasts run
No' for fun
And we lean on window-sill.

Shadows and daurks
Branches and forks
But you there for them to see;
Wee birds chirp
Chirp, chirp
Wi' you still and daurk in the tree!

Duncan Glen

Robin

If on a frosty morning
the robin redbreast calls
his waistcoat red and burning
like a beggar at your walls

throw bread crumbs on the grass for him
when the ground is hard and still
for in his breast there is a flame
that winter cannot kill.

Iain Crichton Smith

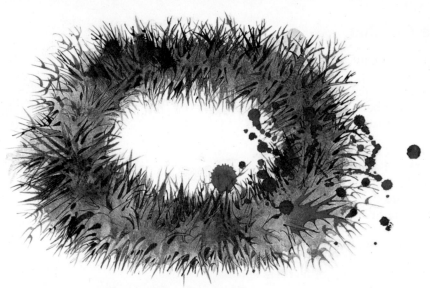

Villanelle de Noel

The robin owre aa birds is blest
At this time o' the year, Noel:
The bluid o' Christ is on his breast.

Frae Sicily ti Hammerfest
The bairns relate the sely tale:
The robin owre aa birds is blest.

For on Calvarie he tried to wrest
Frae Yeshu's palm the cruel nail:
The bluid o' Christ is on his breast.

Sensyne he's been Yuill's dearest guest,
Nae ither sae welcome as himsel':
The robin owre aa birds is blest.

He wears the Yuilltide like a vest
And his sang's the peal o' a ferlie bell.
The bluid o' Christ is on his breast.

Nae starred and medalled hero's chest
Can e'er wi' greater merit swell.
The robin owre aa birds is blest.
The bluid o' Christ is on his breast.

Tom Scott

The Combat

It was not meant for human eyes,
That combat on the shabby patch
Of clods and trampled turf that lies
Somewhere beneath the sodden skies
For eye of toad or adder to catch.

And having seen it I accuse
The crested animal in his pride,
Arrayed in all the royal hues
Which hide the claws he well can use
To tear the heart out of the side.

Body of leopard, eagle's head
And whetted beak, and lion's mane,
And frost-grey hedge of feathers spread
Behind—he seemed of all things bred.
I shall not see his like again.

As for his enemy, there came in
A soft round beast as brown as clay:
All rent and patched his wretched skin;
A battered bag he might have been,
Some old used thing to throw away.

Yet he awaited face to face
The furious beast and the swift attack.
Soon over and done. That was no place
Or time for chivalry or for grace.
The fury had him on his back.

And two small paws like hands flew out
To right and left as the trees stood by.
One would have said beyond a doubt
This was the very end of the bout,
But that the creature would not die.

For ere the death-stroke he was gone,
Writhed, whirled, huddled into his den,
Safe somehow there. The fight was done,
And he had lost who had all but won.
But oh his deadly fury then.

A while the place lay blank, forlorn,
Drowsing as in relief from pain.
The cricket chirped, the grating thorn
Stirred, and a little sound was born.
The champions took their posts again.

And all began. The stealthy paw
Slashed out and in. Could nothing save
These rags and tatters from the claw?
Nothing. And yet I never saw
A beast so helpless and so brave.

And now, while the trees stand watching, still
The unequal battle rages there.
The killing beast that cannot kill
Swells and swells in his fury till
You'd almost think it was despair.

Edwin Muir

The Twa Corbies

As I was walking all alane,
I heard twa corbies making a mane;
The tane unto the t'other say,
'Where sall we gan and dine to-day?'—

'In behint yon auld fail dyke,
I wot there lies a new-slain knight;
And naebody kens that he lies there,
But his hawk, his hound, and lady fair.

'His hound is to the hunting gane,
His hawk, to fetch the wild-fowl hame,
His lady's ta'en another mate,
Sa we may mak our dinner sweet.

'Ye'll sit on his white hause-bane,
And I'll pick out his bonny blue een:
Wi' ae lock o' his gowden hair,
We'll theek our nest when it grows bare.

'Mony a one for him makes mane,
But nane sall ken where he is gane:
O'er his white banes, when they are bare,
The wind sall blaw for evermair,'—

Anon.

The Bonny Butcher

It is the bonny butcher lad
   That wears the sleeves of blue,
He sells the flesh on Saturday,
   On Friday that he slew.

Sir Walter Scott

The Christmas Goose

Mr Smiggs was a gentleman,
  And he lived in London town;
His wife she was a good kind soul,
  And seldom known to frown.

'Twas on Christmas eve,
  And Smiggs and his wife lay cosy in bed,
When the thought of buying a goose
  Came into his head.

So the next morning,
  Just as the sun rose,
He jump'd out of bed,
  And he donn'd his clothes,

Saying, 'Peggy, my dear,
  You need not frown,
For I'll buy you the best goose
  In all London town.'

So away to the poultry shop he goes,
  And he bought the goose, as he did propose,
And for it he paid one crown,
  The finest, he thought, in London town.

When Smiggs bought the goose
  He suspected no harm,
But a naughty boy stole it
  From under his arm.

Then Smiggs he cried, 'Stop, thief!
    Come back with my goose!'
But the naughty boy laugh'd at him,
    And gave him much abuse.

But a policeman captur'd the naughty boy,
    And gave the goose to Smiggs,
And said he was greatly bother'd
    By a set of juvenile prigs.

So the naughty boy was put in prison
    For stealing the goose,
And got ten days' confinement
    Before he got loose.

So Smiggs ran home to his dear Peggy,
    Saying, 'Hurry, and get this fat goose ready,
That I have bought for one crown;
    So, my darling, you need not frown.'

'Dear Mr Smiggs, I will not frown;
    I'm sure 'tis cheap for one crown,
Especially at Christmas time—
    Oh! Mr Smiggs, it's really fine.'

'Peggy, it is Christmas time,
    So let us drive dull care away,
For we have got a Christmas goose,
    So cook it well, I pray.

'No matter how the poor are clothed,
    Or if they starve at home,
We'll drink our wine, and eat our goose,
    Aye, and pick it to the bone.'

William McGonagall

Loss

A tulip fell deid
bi ma doorstep the day
dark rid the colour o' blood.
    Wis the only yin come up this year.
    A imagine it fell wi' a thud.

Alan Jackson

Lord Randal

'O where ha you been, Lord Randal, my son?
And where ha you been, my handsome young man?'
'I ha been at the greenwood; mother, mak my bed soon,
For I'm wearied wi' huntin', and fain wad lie down.'

'An' wha met ye there, Lord Randal, my son?
An' wha met you there, my handsome young man?'
'O I met wi' my true-love; mother, mak my bed soon,
For I'm wearied wi' huntin', and fain wad lie down.'

'And what did she give you, Lord Randal, my son?
And what did she give you, my handsome young man?'
'Eels fried in a pan; mother, mak my bed soon,
For I'm wearied wi' huntin', and fain wad lie down.'

'And wha gat your leavins, Lord Randal, my son?
And wha gat your leavins, my handsome young man?'
'My hawks and my hounds; mother, mak my bed soon,
For I'm wearied wi' huntin', and fain wad lie down.'

'And what becam of them, Lord Randal, my son?
And what becam of them, my handsome young man?'
'They stretched their legs out an died; mother, mak my bed
      soon,
For I'm wearied wi' huntin', and fain wad lie down.'

'O I fear you are poisoned, Lord Randal, my son!
I fear you are poisoned, my handsome young man!'
'O yes, I am poisoned; mother, mak my bed soon,
For I'm sick at the heart, and I fain wad lie down.'

'What d'ye leave to your mother, Lord Randal, my son?
What d'ye leave to your mother, my handsome young man?'
'Four and twenty milk kye; mother, mak my bed soon,
For I'm sick at the heart, and I fain wad lie down.'

'What d'ye leave to your sister, Lord Randal, my son?
What d'ye leave to your sister, my handsome young man?'
'My gold and my silver; mother, mak my bed soon,
For I'm sick at the heart, and I fain wad lie down.'

'What d'ye leave to your brother, Lord Randal, my son?
What d'ye leave to your brother, my handsome young man?'
'My houses and my lands; mother, mak my bed soon,
For I'm sick at the heart, and I fain wad lie down.'

'What d'ye leave to your true-love, Lord Randal, my son?
What d'ye leave to your true-love, my handsome young man?'
'I leave her hell and fire; mother, mak my bed soon,
For I'm sick at the heart, and I fain wad lie down.'

Anon.

My Banes

My banes are buried in yon kirk-yard
   Sae far ayont the sea,
And it is but my blithesome ghaist
   That's speaking now to thee.

Sir Walter Scott

The Witches

In crooked cottages the witches dwell.
They get their water from the crooked well
and crooked smoke from crooked chimneys rise
and if you look you'll see they have crooked eyes.

In crooked woods by crooked paths they go
with crooked feet among the crooked snow
leaving their crooked shadows on the ground
with crooked cat and crooked crooked hound.

On crooked paper they write crooked names.
At crooked birds they take their crooked aims.
And when it's midnight they lay crooked heads
on the crooked pillows of their crooked beds.

Iain Crichton Smith

The Fause Knight and the Wee Boy

'O where are ye gaun?'
  Quo' the fause knight upon the road;
'I'm gaun to the schule,'
  Quo' the wee boy, and still he stude.

'What is that upon your back?'
  Quo' the fause knight upon the road;
'Atweel it is my bukes,'
  Quo' the wee boy, and still he stude.

'What's that ye've got in your arm?'
  Quo' the fause knight upon the road;
'Atweel it is my peat,'
  Quo' the wee boy, and still he stude.

'Wha's aucht thae sheep?'
  Quo' the fause knight upon the road,
'They're mine and my mother's,'
  Quo' the wee boy, and still he stude.

'How mony o' them are mine?'
  Quo' the fause knight upon the road;
'A' they that hae blue tails,'
  Quo' the wee boy, and still he stude.

'I wiss ye were on yon tree,'
  Quo' the fause knight upon the road;
'And a guid ladder under me,'
  Quo' the wee boy, and still he stude.

'And the ladder for to break,'
  Quo' the fause knight upon the road;
'And you for to fa' down,'
  Quo' the wee boy, and still he stude.

'I wiss ye were in yon sea,'
  Quo' the fause knight upon the road;
'And a guid bottom under me,'
  Quo' the wee boy, and still he stude.

'And the bottom for to break,'
  Quo' the fause knight upon the road;
'And ye to be drownèd,'
  Quo' the wee boy, and still he stude.

Anon.

The Fairy Man

The nicht is mirk
The hous is toom
O gowls the wund
Atour ma room.

The hous is deid
Daith's sib tae sleep
The rain dings doun
The nicht is deep.

'Come ben, ma dear
Wi' the glentan ee,
Why shud I fear
Whit thou wald dae?'

He's up the stair
But maks nae soun
He's in ma room—
An' the wund dees doun!

He taks ma haun
An' fell's his grin
The souch o his breith's
Lik a rairan lynn.

O cauld's ma hert
O mauch's ma brou
His oorie breith's
Upo' me nou.

'G' awa', g'awa'
Ma fairy man,
Ma hert is cauld
I wald ye'd gang!'

But neer he'll gang
He's aye yir ain
Whan nichts are lang
An thochts are lane.

Sydney Goodsir Smith

Bonnie George Campbell

Hie upon Hielands,
  And laigh upon Tay,
Bonnie George Campbell
  Rode out on a day.

He saddled, he bridled,
  And gallant rode he;
And hame cam his guid horse,
  But never cam he.

Out cam his mother dear,
  Greeting fu' sair;
And out cam his bonnie bride
  Riving her hair.

'The meadow lies green,
  The corn is unshorn;
But bonnie George Campbell
  Will never return.'

Saddled and bridled
  And booted rode he,
A plume in his helmet,
  A sword at his knee:

But toom cam his saddle,
  All bloody to see;
Oh, hame cam his guid horse,
  But never cam he.

Anon.

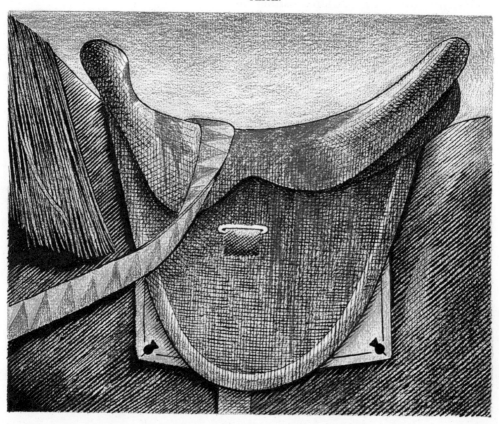

Canadian Boat Song

Fair these broad meads—these hoary woods are grand;
But we are exiles from our fathers' land.

Listen to me, as when ye heard our father
   Sing long ago the song of other shores—
Listen to me, and then in chorus gather
   All your deep voices, as ye pull your oars.

From the lone shieling of the misty island
   Mountains divide us, and the waste of seas—
Yet still the blood is strong, the heart is Highland,
   And we in dreams behold the Hebrides.

We ne'er shall tread the fancy-haunted valley,
   Where 'tween the dark hills creeps the small clear stream,
In arms around the patriarch banner rally,
   Nor see the moon on royal tombstones gleam.

When the bold kindred, in the time long vanish'd,
   Conquer'd the soil and fortified the keep—
No seer foretold the children would be banish'd,
   That a degenerate lord might boast his sheep.

Come foreign rage—let Discord burst in slaughter!
   O then for clansmen true, and stern claymore—
The hearts that would have given their blood like water,
   Beat heavily beyond the Atlantic roar.

Anon.

Lachin Y Gair

Away, ye gay landscapes, ye gardens of roses!
  In you let the minions of luxury rove;
Restore me the rocks where the snow-flake reposes,
  Though still they are sacred to freedom and love:
Yet, Caledonia, beloved are thy mountains,
  Round their white summits though elements war;
Though cataracts foam 'stead of smooth-flowing fountains,
  I sigh for the valley of dark Loch na Garr.

Ah! there my young footsteps in infancy wander'd;
  My cap was the bonnet, my cloak was the plaid;
On chieftains long perish'd my memory ponder'd,
  As daily I strode through the pine-cover'd glade;
I sought not my home till the day's dying glory
  Gave place to the rays of the bright polar star;
For fancy was cheer'd by traditional story,
  Disclos'd by the natives of dark Loch na Garr.

'Shades of the dead! have I not heard your voices
  Rise on the night-rolling breath of the gale?'
Surely the soul of the hero rejoices
  And rides on the wind o'er his own highland vale.
Round Loch na Garr while the stormy mist gathers,
  Winter presides in his cold icy car:
Clouds there encircle the forms of my fathers;
  They dwell in the tempests of dark Loch na Garr.

84

'Ill-starr'd, though brave, did no visions foreboding
   Tell you that fate had forsaken your cause?'
Ah! were you destin'd to die at Culloden,
   Victory crown'd not your fall with applause:
Still were you happy in death's earthly slumber,
   You rest with your clan in the caves of Braemar;
The pibroch resounds to the piper's loud number,
   Your deeds on the echoes of dark Loch na Garr.

Years have roll'd on, Loch na Garr, since I left you,
   Years must elapse ere I tread you again:
Nature of verdure and flowers has bereft you,
   Yet still are you dearer than Albion's plain.
England! thy beauties are tame and domestic
   To one who has roved o'er the mountains afar:
Oh for the crags that are wild and majestic!
   The steep frowning glories of dark Loch na Garr.

George Gordon, Lord Byron

85

Speaking of Scotland

What do you mean when you speak of Scotland?
The grey defeats that are dead and gone
behind the legends each generation
savours afresh, yet can't live on?

Lowland farm with their broad acres
peopling crops? The colder earth
of the North East? Or Highland mountains
shouldering up their rocky dearth?

Inheritance of guilt that our country
has never stood where we feel she should?
A nagging threat of unfinished struggle
somehow forever lost in the blood?

Scotland's a sense of change, an endless
becoming for which there was never a kind
of wholeness or ultimate category.
Scotland's an attitude of mind.

Maurice Lindsay

The Little White Rose

The rose of all the world is not for me.
I want for my part
Only the little white rose of Scotland
That smells sharp and sweet—and breaks the heart.

Hugh MacDiarmid

Scotland

Here in the uplands
The soil is ungrateful
The fields, red with sorrel,
Are stony and bare.
A few trees, wind-twisted—
Or are they but bushes?
Stand stubbornly guarding
A home here and there.

Scooped out like a saucer,
The land lies before me;
The waters, once scattered,
Flow orderly now
Through fields where the ghosts
Of the marsh and the moorland
Still ride the old marches,
Despising the plough.

The marsh and the moorland
Are not to be banished;
The bracken and the heather,
The glory of broom,
Usurp all the balks
And the field's broken fringes.
And claim from the sower
Their portion of room.

This is my country,
The land that begat me,
These windy spaces
Are surely my own.
And those who here toil
In the sweat of their faces
Are flesh of my flesh,
And bone of my bone.

Hard is the day's task
Scotland, stern Mother—
Wherewith at all times
Thy sons have been faced:
Labour by day,
And scant rest in the gloaming
With Want an attendant,
Not lightly outpaced.

Yet do thy children
Honour and love thee.
Harsh is thy schooling,
Yet great is the gain:
True hearts and strong limbs,
The beauty of faces,
Kissed by the wind
And caressed by the rain.

Alexander Gray

The Barren Fig

O Scotland is
The barren fig.
Up, carles, up
And roond it jig.

Auld Moses took
A dry stick and
Instantly it
Floo'ered in his hand.

Pu' Scotland up,
And wha can say
It winna bud
And blossom tae.

A miracle's
Oor only chance.
Up, carles, up
And let us dance!

Hugh MacDiarmid

I'm Neutral

Last nicht in Scotland Street I met a man
that gruppit my lapel—a kinna foreign
cratur he seemed; he tellt me, There's a war on
atween the Lang-nebs and the Big-heid Clan.

I wasna fasht, I took him for a moron,
naething byordnar, but he said, Ye're wan
of thae lang-nebbit folk, and if I can
I'm gaunnae pash ye doun and rype your sporran.

Says he, I'll get a medal for this job;
we're watchan ye, we ken fine what ye're at,
ye're with us or agin us, shut your gob.

He gied a clout that knockit aff my hat,
bawlan, A fecht! Come on, the Big-heid Mob!
Aweill, I caa'd him owre, and that was that.

Robert Garioch

Acrobats

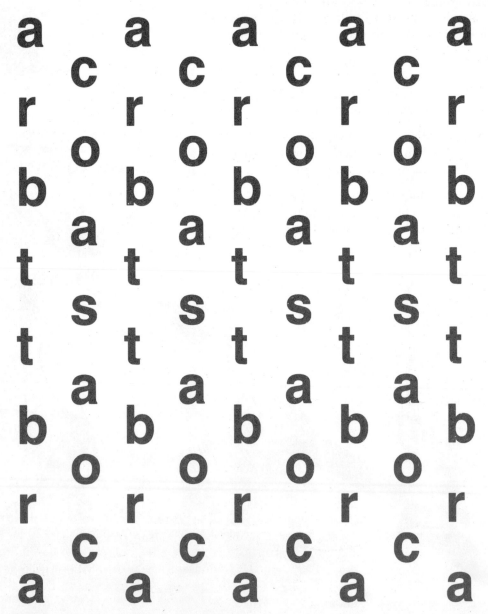

Ian Hamilton Finlay

Glasgow Schoolboys, Running Backwards

High wind ... They turn their backs to it, and push.
Their crazy strides are chopped in little steps.
And all their lives, like that, they'll have to rush
Forwards in reverse, always holding their caps.

Douglas Dunn

Wifie

This wifie wi' a shoppin' basket,
A goes up tae her an' says
Hey wifie, see, there's the wild Pentlands
Just behind ye.

She drapped it.

Alan Jackson

Tradition

'Heh! young folk arena what they were:'
Wheeng'd the auld craw to his cronie:
'Sic galivantin' here and there,
Sic wastrie and aye wantin' mair;
Their menners far frae bonnie.

'Eh me! it's waur and waur they get
In gumption and decorum:
And sma' respec' for kirk or state.'
Wi' that the auld craw wagg'd his pate
As his faither did afore him.

William Soutar

The Beauties of Football

Twisted muscles and broken bones,
Strife, discord and broken homes;
Old players stoop, their bodies stall—
These are the beauties of football.

Anon.

Tinkers

Three princes rigged like scarecrows
Straggled along the shore
And every clucking wife
Ran in and barred her door.

Their coats hung in such shreds
The dogs barked as they came.
O but their steps were a dance,
Their eyes all black flame!

The wife's undone her pack
And spread it at our door.
Grails, emeralds, peacock feathers
Scattered over the floor.

The man flashed his bow,
His fiddle had only one string,
But where is the sun-drowned lark
Like that can sing?

The dark boy wore his rags
Like an April-wakened tree,
Or as a drift of seaweed
Glitters on the arms of the sea.

Princes, they ruled in our street
A long shining age,
While Merran peeped through her curtains
Like a hawk from a cage.

Paupers, they filthied our pier
A piece of one afternoon,
Then scowled, stank, shouldered their packs
And cursed and were gone.

George Mackay Brown

The Tay Bridge Disaster

Beautiful Railway Bridge of the Silv'ry Tay!
Alas! I am very sorry to say
That ninety lives have been taken away
On the last Sabbath day of 1879,
Which will be remember'd for a very long time.

'Twas about seven o'clock at night,
And the wind it blew with all its might,
And the rain came pouring down,
And the dark clouds seem'd to say—
'I'll blow down the Bridge of Tay.'

When the train left Edinburgh
The passengers' hearts were light and felt no sorrow,
But Boreas blew a terrific gale,
Which made their hearts for to quail,
And many of the passengers with fear did say—
'I hope God will send us safe across the Bridge of Tay.'

But when the train came near to Wormit Bay,
Boreas he did loud and angry bray,
And shook the central girders of the Bridge of Tay
On the last Sabbath day of 1879,
Which will be remember'd for a very long time.

So the train sped on with all its might,
And Bonnie Dundee soon hove in sight,
And the passengers' hearts felt light,
Thinking they would enjoy themselves on the New Year,
With their friends at home they lov'd most dear,
And wish them all a happy New Year.

So the train mov'd slowly along the Bridge of Tay,
Until it was about midway,
Then the central girders with a crash gave way,
And down went the train and passengers into the Tay!
The Storm Fiend did loudly bray,
Because ninety lives had been taken away,
On the last Sabbath day of 1879,
Which will be remember'd for a very long time.

As soon as the catastrophe came to be known
The alarm from mouth to mouth was blown,
And the cry rang out all o'er the town,
Good Heavens! the Tay Bridge is blown down,
And a passenger train from Edinburgh,
Which fill'd all the people's hearts with sorrow,
And made them for to turn pale,
Because none of the passengers were sav'd to tell the tale
How the disaster happen'd on the last Sabbath day of 1879,
Which will be remember'd for a very long time.

It must have been an awful sight,
To witness in the dusky moonlight,
While the Storm Fiend did laugh, and angry did bray,
Along the Railway Bridge of the Silv'ry Tay.
Oh! ill-fated Bridge of the Silv'ry Tay.
I must now conclude my lay
By telling the world fearlessly without the least dismay,
That your central girders would not have given way.
At least many sensible men do say,
Had they been supported on each side with buttresses,
At least many sensible men confesses,
For the stronger we our houses do build,
The less chance we have of being killed.

William McGonagall

Song of Pity for Refugees

Snaw is bluffertin' the toun,
Gurly wunds are roustin' roun',
Peety fowk in broken shoon
  This winter nicht.

Peety help the weary auld,
Claes nor fire to fend aff cauld,
Hoose nor ha' them safe to hauld
  This winter nicht.

Peety wham in a' the warld
Fortune fell through hell has harled,
Hungert, hameless, broken, marled,
  This winter nicht.

Peety men withooten kin,
Ne'er a freend to cry them ben,
Nane their deein' sauls to sain
  This winter nicht.

Helen B. Cruickshank

Get Up and Bar the Door

It fell about the Martinmas time,
  And a gay time it was than,
When our gudewife got puddin's to mak,
  And she boil'd them in the pan.

The wind sae cauld blew south and north,
  And blew into the floor:
Quoth our gudeman to our gudewife,
  'Gae out and bar the door.'

'My hand is in my hussif-skep,
  Gudeman, as ye may see,
An it shou'd nae be barr'd this hundred year,
  It's no be barr'd for me.'

They made a paction 'tween them twa,
  They made it firm and sure;
That the first word whae'er shou'd speak,
  Shou'd rise and bar the door.

Then by there came twa gentlemen,
  At twelve o'clock at night,
And they could neither see house nor hall,
  Nor coal nor candle-light.

'Now, whether is this a rich man's house,
  Or whether is it a poor?'
But never a word wad ane o' them speak,
  For barring o' the door.

And first they ate the white puddin's,
  And then they ate the black;
Tho' muckle thought the gudewife to hersel',
  Yet ne'er a word she spak.

Then said the one unto the other,
  'Here, man, tak ye my knife,
Do ye tak aff the auld man's beard,
  And I'll kiss the gudewife.'

'But there's nae water in the house,
    And what shall we do than?'
'What ails you at the puddin' broo,
    That boils into the pan?'

O up then started our gudeman,
    An angry man was he;
'Will ye kiss my wife before my een,
    And scald me wi' puddin' bree?'

Then up and started our gudewife,
    Gied three skips on the floor:
'Gudeman, ye've spoken the foremost word,
    Get up and bar the door.'

Anon.

Tam o' the Linn

Tam o' the linn cam up the gait,
Wi' twenty puddings on a plate,
And every pudding had a pin,
'We'll eat them a',' quo' Tam o' the linn.

Tam o' the linn had nae breeks to wear,
He coft him a sheep's-skin to make him a pair,
The fleshy side out, the woolly side in,
'It's fine summer cleeding,' quo' Tam o' the linn.

Tam o' the linn, he had three bairns,
They fell in the fire, in each other's arms;
'Oh,' quo' the boonmost, 'I've got a het skin';
'It's hetter below,' quo' Tam o' the linn.

Tam o' the linn gaed to the moss,
To seek a stable to his horse;
The moss was open, and Tam fell in,
'I've stabled mysel',' quo' Tam o' the linn.

Anon.

102

Empty Vessel

I met ayont the cairney
A lass wi' tousie hair
Singin' till a bairnie
That was nae langer there.

Wunds wi' warlds to swing
Dinna sing sae sweet,
The licht that bends owre a' thing
Is less ta'en up wi't.

Hugh MacDiarmid

The Eternal Feminine

When I was a freckled bit bairn
　　And cam in frae my ploys to the fire,
Wi' my buits a' clamjamphried wi' shairn
　　And my jaicket a' speldered wi' mire,
I got gloomin' and glunchin' and paiks,
　　And nae bite frae the press or the pan,
And my auld grannie said as she skelped me to bed,
　　'Hech, sirs, what a burden is man!'

104

When I was a lang-leggit lad,
  At waddin's and kirns a gey cheild,
I hae happit a lass in my maud
  And gone cauldrife that she micht hae beild,
And convoyed her bye bogles and stirks,
  A kiss at the hindmost my plan;
But a' that I fand was the wecht o' her hand,
  And 'Hech, sirs, what a burden is man!'

When Ailie and me were made yin
  We set up in a canty bit cot;
Sair wrocht we day oot and day in,
  We were unco content wi' oor lot.
But whiles wi' a neebor I'd tak
  A gless that my heid couldna stan';
Syne she'd greet for a week, and nae word wad she speak
  But 'Hech, sirs, what a burden is man!'

She dee'd, and my dochter and me
  For the lave wi' ilk ither maun shift.
Nae tentier lass could ye see;
  The wooers cam doun like a drift;
But sune wi' an unco bláe glower
  Frae the doorstep they rade and they ran,
And she'd sigh to hersel', as she gae'd to the well,
  'Hech sirs, what a burden is man!'

She's mairrit by noo and she's got
  A white-heided lass o' her ain.
White-heided mysel, as I stot
  Roond the doors o' her shouther I'm fain.
What think ye that wean said yestreen?
  I'll tell ye, believe't if ye can;
She primmed up her mou' and said saft as a doo,
  'Hech, sirs, what a burden is man!'

John Buchan

A Summer's Day

yir eyes ur
eh
a mean yir

pirrit this wey
ah a thingk yir
byewtifil like ehm

fact
fact a thingk yir
ach a luvyi thahts

thahts
jist thi wey it iz like
thahts ehm
aw ther iz ti say

Tom Leonard

August Poem

Today it is raining
and it is autumn.

The children are going back to school with their new bags
and their new uniforms.

It is spring for the children and autumn for the teachers.

For the children are always young and the teachers are
   growing older
and the blackboard is grainy with chalk.

The teachers look out at the rainy playground
and sometimes they think about *Macbeth*
but mostly about their own lives
and how the freshness of spring has departed.

It is raining
and it is autumn,
and the rain prickles the sea
and wets the new uniforms of the children
and their new shoes.

When it is raining the soul becomes grey,
a continuous drizzle of autumn.
It is like a screen that will always be there.

The teachers look out, the forgotten chalk in their hands,
and they break it over and over.

Iain Crichton Smith

ONE (ORANGE) ARM OF THE WORLD'S OLDEST WINDMILL

autumn

Ian Hamilton Finlay

I build an orange church

I build an orange church and put inside it
a little orange minister in a pulpit
that's dandelion yellow.

I make a ceiling of intensest blue.
The seats are heliotrope, the bibles pink,
hymn books are apple green.

Picasso paints the walls with animals.
The angels swoop in red and there's a sun
of blinding nuclear light.

And so transform it all … But for the guilt
that's small and black and creeps in when the door
swings on its oiled hinges.

Iain Crichton Smith

Bawsy Broon

Dinna gang out the nicht:
Dinna gang out the nicht:
Laich was the müne as I cam owre the muir;
Laich was the lauchin' though nane was there:
Somebody nippit me,
Somebody trippit me;
Somebody grippit me roun' and aroun':
I ken it was Bawsy Broon:
I'm shair it was Bawsy Broon.

Dinna win out the nicht:
Dinna win out the nicht:
A rottan reeshl'd as I ran be the sike,
And the dead-bell dunnl'd owre the auld kirk-dyke:
Somebody nippit me,
Somebody trippit me;
Somebody grippit me roun' and aroun':
I ken it was Bawsy Broon:
I'm shair it was Bawsy Broon.

William Soutar

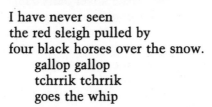

Catherine in Russia

I have never seen
the red sleigh pulled by
four black horses over the snow.
    gallop gallop
    tchrrik tchrrik
    goes the whip

I have never seen
the countess and the prince in
the red sleigh pulled by
four black horses over the snow
    Yo! ho!
    gallop gallop
    tchrrik tchrrik
    goes the whip

I have never seen
the little girl with moon-lit eyes
between the countess and the prince in
the red sleigh pulled by
four black horses over the snow.
    Ho! ho!
    Yo! ho!
    gallop gallop
    tchrrik tchrrik
    goes the whip

I have never seen
the yellow reins run from the pink hands of
the little girl with moon-lit eyes
between the countess and the prince in
the red sleigh pulled by
four black horses over the snow.
    Huzza! Huzza!
    Ho! ho!
    Yo! ho!
    gallop gallop
    tchrrik tchrrik
    goes the whip

I have never seen
the silver bells dance and sing as
the yellow reins run from the pink hands of
the little girl with moon-lit eyes
between the countess and the prince in
the red sleigh pulled by
four black horses over the snow.
    Ching ching
    Huzza! Huzza!
    Ho! ho!
    Yo! ho!
    gallop gallop
    tchrrik tchrrik
    goes the whip

I have never seen
the wild stars call into the skies
the silver bells that dance and sing
the yellow reins and the pink hands and
the little girl with moon-lit eyes
and the countess and the prince in
the red sleigh pulled by
four black horses over the snow.
    Aah-starisk astarisk
    Ching ching
    Huzza! Huzza!
    Ho! ho!
    Yo! ho!
    Gallop gallop
    tchrrik tchrrik
    goes the whip

George Bruce

Lullaby

A

   . . . blue boat
   a brown sail

LITTLE POEM

   a brown boat
   a green sail

TO PUT

   a green boat
   a black sail

YOUR EYES

   a black boat
   a blue sail

TO SLEEP

   a . . .

LITTLE . . .

Ian Hamilton Finlay

On Not Counting Sheep

Seven apple trees, a willow and a pine
At the top of the garden, that makes nine.
A privet and a cypress, a winter-flowering cherry,
A birch and a rowan, green tassel, crimson berry.
A juniper, a hazel, a laurel and a gean.
A yellow rose, a plum-tree, with no plums to glean.
I'm counting my trees; no, I'm not counting sheep –

A rowan at the gateway,

I'm _____ falling _____ asleep.

Helen B. Cruickshank

81

A long moonrise ago
when the world was eighty one
when there were no porpoises and no anteaters
only hot and run
a simple ball without mud or water
in the waves that make space
how cool it must have been
while fire kept it clean
when there was no rain of blood
and no shoes to walk
        over earthflesh

Alan Jackson

Escape at Bedtime

The lights from the parlour and kitchen shone out
   Through the blinds and the windows and bars;
And high overhead and all moving about,
   There were thousands of millions of stars.
There ne'er were such thousands of leaves on a tree,
   Nor of people in church or the Park,
As the crowds of the stars that looked down upon me
   And that glittered and winked in the dark.

The Dog, and the Plough, and the Hunter, and all,
   And the star of the sailor, and Mars,
These shone in the sky, and the pail by the wall
   Would be half full of water and stars.
They saw me at last, and they chased me with cries,
   And they soon had me packed into bed;
But the glory kept shining and bright in my eyes,
   And the stars going round in my head.

Robert Louis Stevenson

The Day the World Ended

for John Betjeman

The washing machine was whirling away,
    The cat was licking its tail,
A pile of clothes was on top and done,
    And a pile was below in a pail.

The basement was growing steamy and warm,
    The cat was alert and wise,
The dryer was doing its job quite well,
    And the jeans were rattling their flies.

The regular wash was all clean and dry,
    The *Tide* was back on the sink,
The handkerchiefs were all fresh and smooth,
    And the towels looked bright and pink.

The revolving drum had come to a halt,
    The shirts were all shut inside,
The air was thick with the smell of suds,
    And the cat's eyes were open wide.

The world was travelling round the sun,
    The moon was out in the West,
A spider was tottering over the floor,
    And the maid was wringing a vest.

The hangers were on the clothes horse,
    The socks were dripping and wet,
The cat had gone for a plate of fish,
    And the sun had started to set.

The light was up in the living-room,
    The lamp was down in the hall,
The cat was hunting a brown rat,
    And nothing had happened at all.

George MacBeth

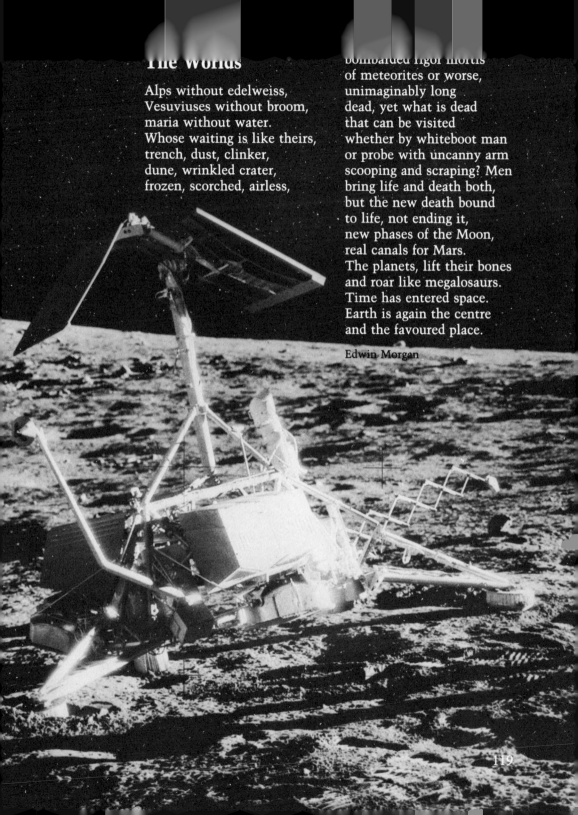

The Worlds

Alps without edelweiss,
Vesuviuses without broom,
maria without water.
Whose waiting is like theirs,
trench, dust, clinker,
dune, wrinkled crater,
frozen, scorched, airless,
bombarded rigor mortis
of meteorites or worse,
unimaginably long
dead, yet what is dead
that can be visited
whether by whiteboot man
or probe with uncanny arm
scooping and scraping? Men
bring life and death both,
but the new death bound
to life, not ending it,
new phases of the Moon,
real canals for Mars.
The planets, lift their bones
and roar like megalosaurs.
Time has entered space.
Earth is again the centre
and the favoured place.

Edwin Morgan

The Planets

All the planets have been named
after the gods, but one at birth
seemed so shy and so ashamed
they simply called it Earth.

But there's this difference between
these godlike planets and our own
though they shine with lovely sheen
they are lifeless lands of stone.

Iain Crichton Smith

120

The sun is burning

The sun is burning in the sky
Strands of cloud are gently drifting by
In the park the dreamy bees
are droning in the flowers among the trees
And the sun burns in the sky

Now the sun is in the west
Little kids lie down to take their rest
And the couples in the park
are holding hands and waiting for the dark
And the sun is in the west

Now the sun is sinking low
Children playing know it's time to go
High above a spot appears
a little blossom blooms and then drops near
And the sun is sinking low

Now the sun has come to earth
Shrouded in a mushroom cloud of death
Death comes in a blinding flash
of hellish heat, and leaves a smear of ash
When the sun has come to earth.

Now the sun has disappeared
All is darkness, anger, pain and fear
Twisted sightless wrecks of men
go groping on their knees and cry in pain
And the sun has disappeared.

Ian Campbell

The Bonnie Broukit Bairn

Mars is braw in crammasy,
Venus in a green silk goun,
The auld mune shak's her gowden feathers,
Their starry talk's a wheen o' blethers,
Nane for thee a thochtie sparin',
Earth, thou bonnie broukit bairn!
—*But greet, an' in your tears ye'll droun*
The haill clanjamfrie!

Hugh MacDiarmid

122

Glossary of Scots Words

Sir Patrick Spens
braid: broad
yestreen: last night
weet: wet
cork-heild: cork-heeled
owre: over
aboone: above
kems: combs

Me
ettles: intends
gar: make
thole: suffer

Basking Shark
slounge: splash
shoggled: jolted

The Whistle
rodden-tree: rowan tree
teuchat: lapwing
puddocks: frogs
herd: boy who tends cattle
kye: cows
kitlin: kitten
syne: since
boss: snug
doit: small coin
clawed: cleaned
caup: dish
lave: remainder
travise: division between
    stall in cowshed
baillie: man in charge of
    cows
marrow: match
dirlin: piercing
halflin: apprentice
spring: lively tune
wistna: knew not
ream: cream
rants: romps

schottisches ⎫
reels   ⎬ dances
jigs   ⎭
futt'rat: weasel
youkie: restless
dool: sorrow
sough: say
catechis: catechism
lickit: beaten
brunt: burnt

*Odd Goings-On in
Dunfermline Town*
heilster gowdie: head over
    heels
puckle: small amount
speirs: asks

Prince Marmaduke
trauchle: struggle

*The Twa Cats and the
Cheese*
kebuck: cheese
skaith: harm
campsho: stern
pales: tests by cutting
prives: examines
ilk: each
knoost: large lump
teughly: energetically
tenting: seeing
daffine: folly
nignyes: trifles
decreet: legal decision

To a Mouse
bickering brattle: nervous
    movement and noise
pattle: ploughstaff
daimen-icker: stray ear of
    corn

thrave: sheaf
lave: remainder
big: build
thole: suffer
cranreuch: frosty
no thy lane: not
    alone

To a Louse
ferlie: wonder
haffet: whisker
squattle: settle down
sprattle: scramble
fatt'rels: ribbons
grozet: gooseberry
rozet: resin
fell, red smeddum: deadly
    powder
droddum: backside
flainen: flannel
aiblins: maybe
duddie: ragged
wylecoat: under vest
blastie: dwarf

The Diseased Salmon
fozie: diseased
bracks: waves
wee: short time
syne: then
tint: lost

The Twa Corbies
corbie: crow or raven
making a mane:
    complaining
fail: turf
theek: thatch

Villanelle de Noel
sely: happy
ferlie: strange

124

My Banes
ayont: beyond
blithesome: merry

The Fairy Man
toom: empty
gowls: howls
souch: moan
rairan lynn: roaring
    waterfall
mauch: damp
oorie: ghostly

Bonnie George Campbell
hie: high
laigh: low
toom: empty

The Barren Fig
carle: man

I'm Neutral
langnebs: long noses
fasht: vexed
byordnar: special

Song of Pity for Refugees
gurly: stormy
harled: dragged
sain: consecrate

Get Up and Bar the Door
hussif-skep: housewifery

Tam o' the Linn
coft: bought or
    bartered
boonmost: topmost

Empty Vessel
wunds: winds
warlds: worlds

The Eternal Feminine
clanjamphried: collected
shairn: cowdung
gloomin': frowning
glunchin': moodiness
paiks: smacks
press: cupboard
kirns: celebrations
gey child: wild young man
happit: covered
maud: plaid
caudrife: chilly
beild: shelter
unco: very
tentier: more attractive
blae glower: blank
    disappointed look
shouther: shoulder
fain: fond
doo: dove

Bawsy Broon
laich: low
rottan: rat
reeshl'd: scurried
sike: rill
dunnl'd: clanged

The Bonnie Broukit Bairn
crammasy: crimson
wheen: lot
clanjamfrie: collection/
    rowdy collection of
    people

Index of First Lines

126

Acknowledgements

The Editor and Publisher wish to thank the following for permission to reprint copyright poems in this anthology.

J.K. Annand: 'Come Sailin' from *Thrice to Show Ye* (Macdonald Publishers). Reprinted by permission of the author.   Robin Bell: 'Hares Boxing' from *Sawing Logs* (Workshop Press Ltd.). Reprinted by permission of the author.   Alan Bold: 'Ballad of the Flat Earth'. Reprinted by permission of the author.   George Mackay Brown: 'The Black Horseman' is previously unpublished and is reprinted by permission of the author. 'Tinkers', from *Poems New and Selected* is reprinted by permission of The Hogarth Press Ltd., for the author.   George Bruce: 'Catherine in Russia' and 'Odd Goings-on in Dunfermline Toun'. Reprinted by permission of the author.   John Buchan: 'The Eternal Feminine'. Reprinted by permission of Lord Tweedsmuir and A.P. Watt Ltd.   Tom Buchan: 'The Seagulls' from *Dolphins at Cochin*, © Tom Buchan 1969, published by Barrie & Jenkins (London) and Hill & Wang (New York). Reprinted by permission of the author.   Donald Campbell: 'Prince Marmaduke . . .', © 1981 Donald Campbell. Reprinted by permission of the author.   Ian Campbell: 'The Sun is Burning'. Reprinted by permission of the author.   Helen B. Cruickshank: 'On Not Counting Sheep' and 'Song of Pity for Refugees' from *Collected Poems* (ed. Gordon Wright). Reprinted by permission of Gordon Wright Publishing.   Douglas Dunn: 'Glasgow schoolboys . . .' from *Barbarians*. Reprinted by permission of Faber & Faber Ltd.   Ian Hamilton Finlay: 'The Cloud's Anchor', 'Acrobats', 'One (Orange) Arm of the World's Oldest Windmill' and 'Lullaby', from *Poems to Hear and See* (Macmillan). Reprinted by permission of the author.   Robert Garioch: 'I'm Neutral' from *Collected Poems* (Macdonald Publishers/Carcanet, 1980). Reprinted by permission of the author.   Duncan Glen: 'To the Houlet'. Reprinted by permission of the author.   W.S. Graham: 'The Beast in the Space' from *Collected Poems 1942–1977* (Faber). Reprinted by permission of the author.   Alexander Gray: 'Scotland'. Reprinted by permission of John Gray.   J.F. Hendry: 'Catfish', 'Crab' and 'Porcupine' from *Who's Zoo*. Reprinted by permission of the author.   Alan Jackson: 'Loss', 'Wifie' and '81'. Reprinted by permission of the author. R.D. Laing: 'I dreamt I was a butterfly' and 'sometimes I come' from *Do You Really Love Me*? (Allen Lane/Penguin Books, 1977) p. 37. Copyright © R.D. Laing, 1976. Reprinted by permission of Penguin Books Ltd. Tom Leonard: 'A Summer's Day' from *Bunnit Hesslin* (Pluralist Press). Reprinted by permission of the author.   Maurice Lindsay: 'Speaking of Scotland' from *Collected Poems* (Paul Harris Publishing, 1979). 'Ballad of the Hare', © 1981 Maurice Lindsay. Both reprinted by permission of the author.   George MacBeth: 'The Day the World Ended' from *Poems of Love and Death*. Reprinted by permission of Martin Secker & Warburg Ltd.   Norman MacCaig: 'Basking Shark' from *A Man in My Position*. 'Frogs' from *Surroundings*. Reprinted by permission of The Hogarth Press Ltd., for the author. 'Jumping Toad' is previously unpublished and reprinted by permission of the author.   Hugh MacDiarmid: 'The Bonnie Broukit Bairn', 'Empty Vessel', 'The Barren Fig', 'The Little White Rose', 'The Ross-shire Hills', 'The Diseased Salmon' and 'Me', all from *The Complete Poems of Hugh MacDiarmid 1920–1976*. Reprinted by permission of the publishers Martin Brian & O'Keefe Ltd., and Mrs. Valda Grieve.   Edwin Morgan: 'The Worlds' from *Star Gate* (Third Eye Centre, Glasgow). Reprinted by permission of the author.   Edwin Muir: 'The Combat' and 'The Late Wasp' from *The Collected Poems of Edwin Muir*. Reprinted by permission of Faber & Faber Ltd.   Charles Murray: 'The Whistle' from *Hamewith* (The Aberdeen University Press Ltd.). Reprinted by permission of the Executors of the late Charles Murray.   Allan Ramsay: 'The Twa Cats and the Cheese' reprinted from *The Works of Allan Ramsay*, Vol. II by permission of The Scottish Text Society.   Alan Riddell: 'The Three Voyages . . . of Captain Cook' and 'The Honey Pot', from *Eclipse*. Reprinted by permission of John Calder (Publishers) Ltd.   Tom Scott: 'Villanelle de Noel'. First appeared in *The Scotsman*. Reprinted by permission of the author.   Iain Crichton Smith: 'I build an orange church' from *Selected Poems*. Reprinted by permission of Victor Gollancz Ltd. 'The Moon', 'The Rainbow', 'Spelling Game', 'Robin', 'The Witches' and 'The Planets', all previously unpublished. 'August Poem' first appeared in *Writers in Brief*, No. 8. All reprinted by permission of the author.   Sydney Goodsir Smith: 'The Fairy Man' from *Collected Poems*. Reprinted by permission of John Calder (Publishers) Ltd.   William Soutar: 'Tradition' and 'Bawsy Broon', from *Poems in Scots and English* by William Soutar, edited by Dr. W.R. Aitken (Scottish Academic Press). Reprinted by permission of The Trustees of The National Library of Scotland.